WELCOME TO EARTH!

by
Darrin Drda

ISBN: 1515163903
ISBN-13: 978-1515163909
Amargi Media

Welcome to Earth!
We're so thrilled that you're here!
We hope you had a nice birth,
and are enjoying your first years.

YOU ARE HERE

I'm Gaia, Earth Mother,
and I'll be your guide.
There's so much to discover,
so let's look inside!

The Earth is a planet.
From space, it looks like a ball.
But when closely examined,
its face is not smooth at all!

Earth has mountains, and deserts,
and forests with trees.
It has valleys with rivers
that run to the sea!

If we take a closer look
at each of these features,
in every cranny and nook,
we'll find marvelous creatures!

Some swim in the water.
Some fly in the sky.
Others crawl, hop, or walk
on the land where it's dry.

Millions of life forms
wearing scales, fur, and feathers
to help keep them warm
in all kinds of weather.

Out of all of these beings,
only one kind wears clothes.
Can you guess? Yes, it's humans!
And you're one of those!

Human beings are animals, and they're very unique. They're non-hairy mammals that walk on two feet!

With clever hands and brains,
humans know how to build things,
like cars, trucks, and planes,
and cities with buildings.

Yes, people are smart,
but that's just the start!
They also make art
that comes from the heart.

They write poems and books,
act in plays, dance, and sing,
play instruments and cook,
and do lots of other things!

Almost anything you can imagine,
humans can be and create.
Yet it's their care and compassion
that make them extra great!

For there is beauty beyond measure,
underneath the sky above,
but by far the greatest treasure
that you'll ever find is

LOVE.

Yes, Earth is full of wonderful things,
and one of them is YOU!

So I wonder, my dear earthling...

**What on earth will
YOU be and do?**

Made in the USA
Las Vegas, NV
16 October 2021